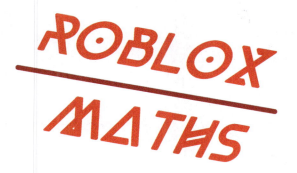

CONTENTS

I'D RATHER BE PLAYING ROBLOX

GamerFan22 creates an awesome new avatar and is left with a ⬡ total of **three thousand six hundred and twenty.**

Write out their ⬡ total using numbers.

Friends are comparing their ⬡ totals;

List these numbers in order from smallest to largest.

Robodude – 8092

TwinkleS – 8120

ElitePlus – 6320

Untalkable – 5000

PrestonS – 6100

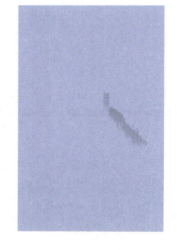

Write out ElitePlus's total using words.

◻ NUMBER AND PLACE VALUE

You are playing Adopt Me, it's an October Halloween update. You and other players purchase a Shadow Dragon game pass for ⬡ 1000 from the Candy Trading Shop.

How many ⬡ do you and the other players have left?

You	2200	−1000
MrBoost	7830	−1000
Sean100	1350	−1000
PinkGamer	9990	−1000

PinkGamer wants to buy 1 Royal Egg and 2 Pink Eggs. Royal eggs are ⬡ 1450 and pink eggs are ⬡ 100.

$$1450$$
$$+ 100$$
$$+ 100$$

What is the total ⬡ cost?

◻ NUMBER AND PLACE VALUE

 Work at a pizza place

Each item on the menu costs ◉ 100

Player 1, 2 and 3's total spends have been entered incorrectly on the till! Your manager has asked you to round them to the **nearest 100**.

	Total	New Total
Player 1	540	
Player 2	250	
Player 3	955	

COUNT IN MULTIPLES

Chance to win lucky blocks in The Floor is Lava!

Get the 6 digit winning codes by finding the 3 multiples of each number and entering them into the boxes provided!

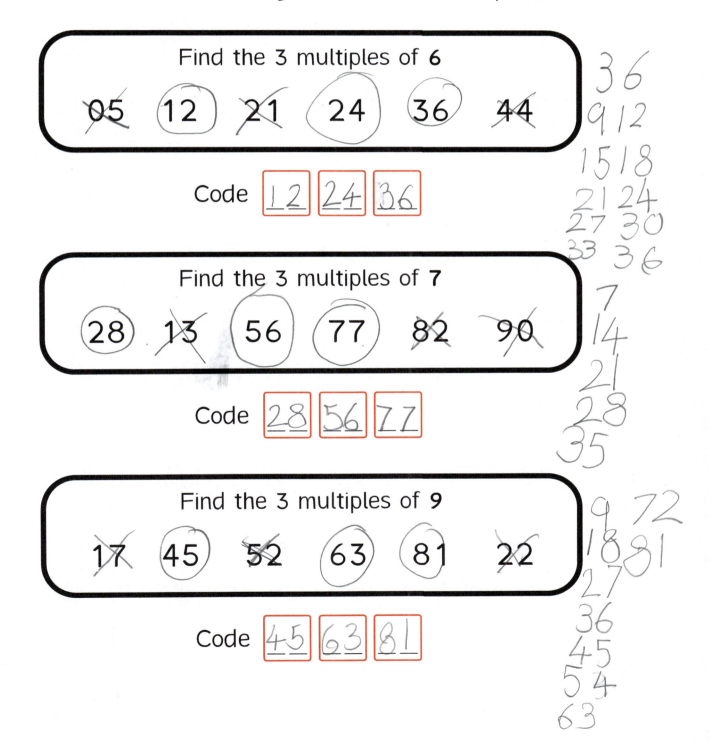

Find the 3 multiples of **6**

05   (12)   21   (24)   (36)   44

Code 12 24 36

Find the 3 multiples of **7**

(28)   13   (56)   (77)   82   90

Code 28 56 77

Find the 3 multiples of **9**

17   (45)   52   (63)   (81)   22

Code 45 63 81

(margin working):
36
9 12
15 18
21 24
27 30
33 36

7
14
21
28
35

9   72
18   81
27
36
45
54
63

COUNT IN MULTIPLES

You've got unlimited 25 skips in the Mega Easy Obby 750 stages.

Count to 750 in multiples of 25.
Fill in the missing stages.

25,___,___, 100, 125,___,___, 200,

225,___,___, 300,___,___,___, 400,

425,___,___,___,___, 550,___,___,

625,___,___, 700, ___ , ___

750

ROMAN NUMERALS

[Building] Empire Roleplay

Your map has 100 forts to help defend your emperor! To command your troops you need to know the Roman Numeral for each fort.

Fill in the missing Roman Numerals on the 100 square below.

I				V					X
			XIV	XV				XIX	
XXI							XXVIII		
	XXXII					XXXVII			XL
		XLIII						XLIX	L
					LVI				
LXI							LXVIII		LXX
			LXXIV			LXXVII			
	LXXXII							LXXXIX	XC
		XCIII	XCIV	XCV		XCVII			C

◨ ROMAN NUMERALS

A member of your troop has stolen your opponents map so you can see which forts they are planning to strike.

BUT, they have used numbers!

Use your 100 square to help you find the Roman Numeral equivalent.

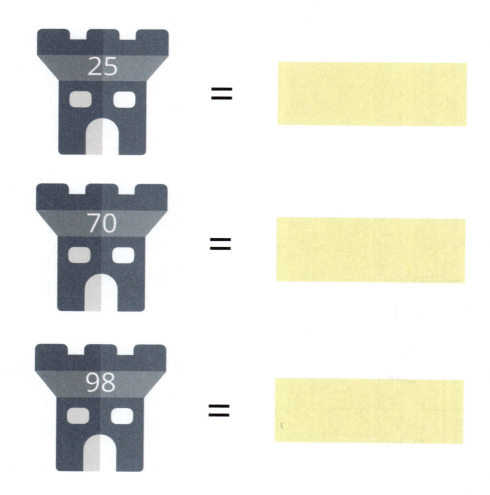

25 =

70 =

98 =

Goal: Build a shape obby.

How: Collect the information below needed for coding.

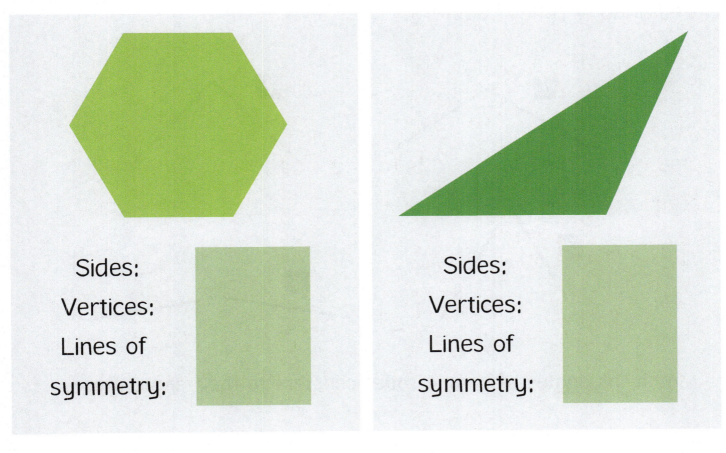

Sides:

Vertices:

Lines of symmetry:

Sides:

Vertices:

Lines of symmetry:

Shape Sudoku

Place these 6 shapes into the blank spaces so that each row, column and **2x2 box** contains one of each shape without repeats.

Time to play Theme Park Tycoon 2, you've got your own plot of land to build your theme park on and you have designed 4 roller coasters.

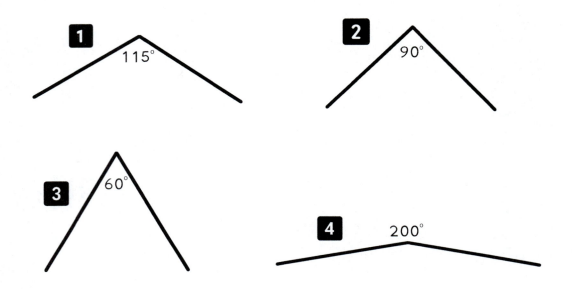

Match the angles of your 4 roller coasters to their angle types.

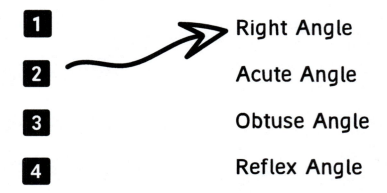

List the angles from **smallest** to **largest**.

◻ ANGLES & COORDINATES

Blue team has got some cannons lined up on

Pilfering Pirates!

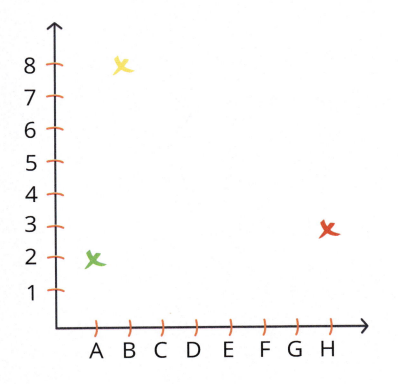

Using the graph, list the coordinates of the 3 ships blue team are aiming for.

The sea is stormy, the boats have moved.

Plot their new coordinates on the graph.

×   B,7

×   A,5

×   F,3

Which colour boat moved the furthest from their original position?

[Escape the running head]

During the final stages of level 3 you find a green coin and are awarded directions out of the maze!

Follow the instructions below to escape.

Stand still with feet together.

- Turn 2 right angles to the left
- Take 3 step backwards
- Turn 3 right angles to the right
- Take 5 steps forward
- Turn 1 right angle to the left

You've escaped!

MULTIPLICATION

The trucks in [Break In (story)] either carry 6, 8 or 11 players. Complete the multiplication wheels below to see how many players join depending on the number of trucks each day between 1–12.

Multiply the numbers by the middle number!

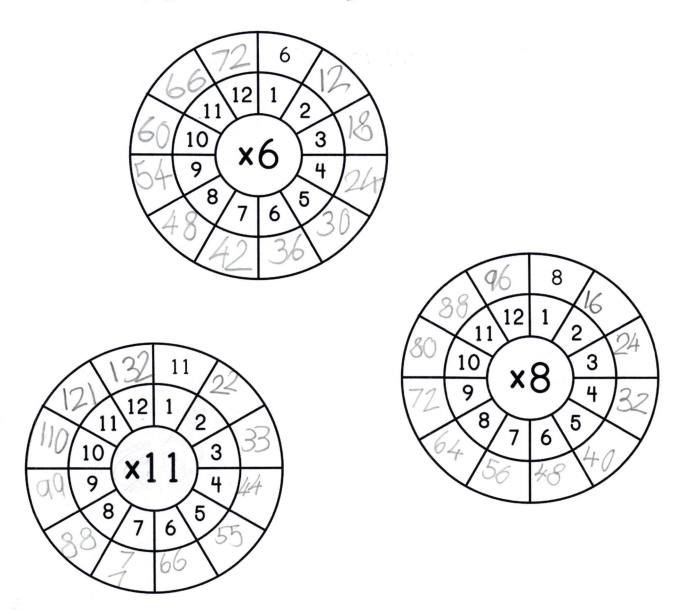

◻ MULTIPLICATION

Challenge:

Give yourself 2 minutes to list as many factor pairs as you can for the numbers below!

36

$1 \times 36 = 36$

$2 \times 18 = 36$

$12 \times 3 = 36$

$6 \times 6 = 36$

$9 \times 4 = 36$

12

$4 \times 3 = 12$

$1 \times 12 = 12$

$2 \times 6 = 12$

52

$1 \times 52 = 52$

$13 \times 4 = 52$

GamerGuy31 gets 80 robux daily for keeping his room tidy, how many does he get per week?

$$\begin{array}{r} 80 \\ \times\ 7 \\ \hline 560 \end{array}$$

Each of GamerGuy31's 8 friends have got 4 pet bees ready to make a neon! How many bees are there in total?

MULTIPLICATION

Repeat: I'd rather be playing Roblox, but I need to practice multiplication!

Complete the questions below.

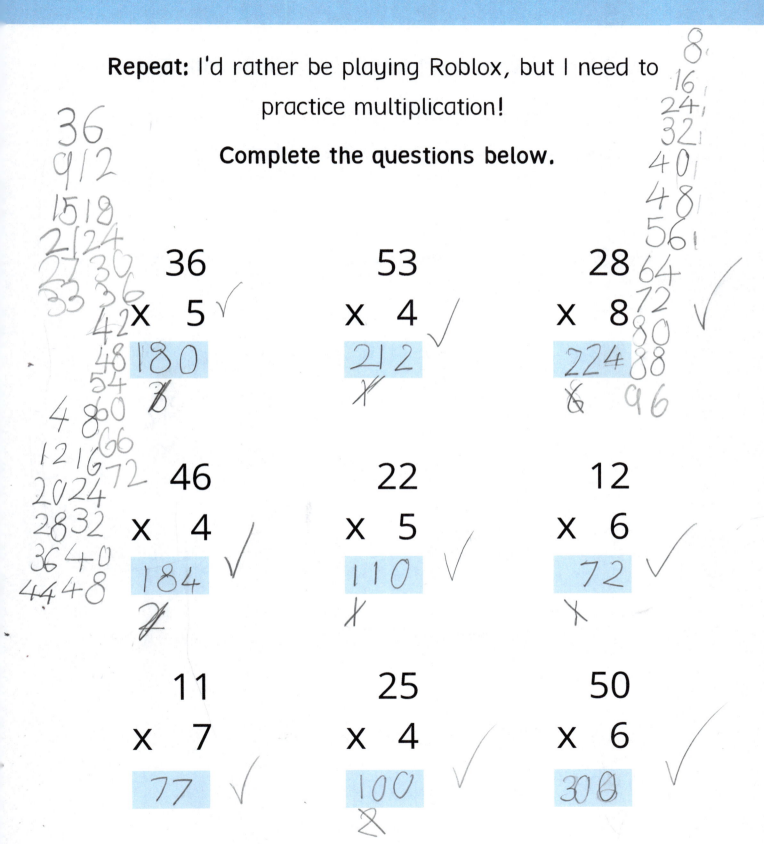

```
   36          53          28
 x  5 ✓      x  4 ✓      x  8 ✓
  180         212         224
```

```
   46          22          12
 x  4 ✓      x  5 ✓      x  6 ✓
  184         110          72
```

```
   11          25          50
 x  7 ✓      x  4 ✓      x  6 ✓
   77         100         300
```

RP : Trapped in the Maths classroom with Baldi.

Baldi won't let you leave until you complete the division questions below.

$60 \div 5 =$ ☐ $24 \div 3 =$ ☐ $48 \div 8 =$ ☐

$6\overline{)66}$ $4\overline{)64}$ $7\overline{)91}$ $3\overline{)72}$

$5\overline{)560}$ $8\overline{)792}$ $3\overline{)336}$ $4\overline{)140}$

There were 32 students in the class, a quarter escaped! How many made it out?

ADDITION AND SUBTRACTION

[Car Crusher 2] Shopping Spree!

You want to add 2 new cars to your collection.

Investigate the total costs of the duo vehicles below.

Cherevlo Airvor **2675**

Golf Cart **5102**

Total Cost

Nyssat Salvio **6375**

Cherevlo Alstra **500**

Total Cost

Forter Fabreville **1550**

Golf Cart **5135**

Total Cost

Fita A50 **8075**

Forter Fabreville **1550**

Total Cost

Rylan MK1 **3324**

Cherevlo Airvor **2675**

Total Cost

Forter Fabreville **1550**

Ford MT **1020**

Total Cost

[Meep City Shop] Pick a side

Subtract the cost of each item listed below from your current coin total of **9780**

Will the answer be on the pink or blue side?
Circle the correct remaining total.

Item	Cost	Coins remaining	
Pogo Stick	3500	6280	6820
Unicycle	2000	7000	7780
Rollerblades	750	9040	9030
Rainbow Sparkler	2500	7280	6280
Mystic Wings	1250	8530	8930
Bee Wings	950	8800	8830

◻ ADDITION AND SUBTRACTION

1500 gamers were asked to pick their favourite game out of Brookhaven, Meep City and Club Roblox.

600 picked Brookhaven, 350 picked Meep City.

How many picked Club Roblox?

Clubbloxerfan has 7500 coins in Don't Press the Button. They spend 650 on a shrinking potion and 6000 on a flying carpet.

How many coins do they have left?

Circle the fraction represented by the black icons.

$$\frac{2}{3} \qquad \frac{1}{2} \qquad \frac{2}{5}$$

The energy bars of 4 players in Blox Fruits are listed in fraction form below. **List them from smallest to largest.**

$$\frac{1}{3} \qquad \frac{1}{10} \qquad \frac{1}{2} \qquad \frac{1}{6}$$

— — — —

Friend 1   Friend 2   Friend 3

6 lucky blocks are to be shared equally between 3 friends.

What fraction of lucky blocks do they each get?

[Pizza Factory Tycoon]

2 friends have visited your restaurant, they want to share a pizza. **Circle all the equivalent fractions of** $\frac{1}{2}$

$$\frac{1}{3} \qquad \frac{2}{4} \qquad \frac{3}{6} \qquad \frac{3}{3}$$

$$\frac{4}{8} \qquad \frac{1}{4} \qquad \frac{4}{6} \qquad \frac{5}{10}$$

More customers arrive, all pizzas are the same size but the number of slices per pizza varies. Calculate the equivalent fractions below to ensure everyone gets the same amount to eat.

$$\frac{1}{2} = \frac{\boxed{}}{6} \qquad\qquad \frac{3}{6} = \frac{\boxed{}}{10} \qquad\qquad \frac{4}{8} = \frac{\boxed{}}{12}$$

$$\frac{1}{3} = \frac{\boxed{}}{6} \qquad\qquad \frac{4}{8} = \frac{\boxed{}}{4} \qquad\qquad \frac{3}{4} = \frac{\boxed{}}{8}$$

⬛ FRACTIONS AND DECIMALS

Add these fractions to find out which table ate a **whole** pizza.

Table 1 $\quad \dfrac{1}{7} + \dfrac{5}{7} \qquad = \dfrac{}{7}$

Table 2 $\quad \dfrac{2}{6} + \dfrac{2}{6} \qquad = \dfrac{}{}$

Table 3 $\quad \dfrac{1}{3} + \dfrac{1}{3} + \dfrac{1}{3} \qquad = \dfrac{}{}$

Table ▢ finished 1 whole pizza.

There is one big sauce dispenser where customers can get their own pizza dipping sauce. Subtract the fraction of sauce used in a day. **What fraction of sauce is left?**

$$\dfrac{2}{5} - \dfrac{1}{5} = \dfrac{}{} \qquad \dfrac{4}{6} - \dfrac{3}{6} = \dfrac{}{}$$

PiggyFan11 and friends are all comparing how much pizza they have eaten, but their pizzas all had different amounts of slices. This means their fractions all have different denominators.

Using the symbols < and > compare the pizza fractions to see who ate the most.

Tip: Draw pizza shapes and shade in the fractions to help you to compare!

$\dfrac{1}{2}$ ☐ $\dfrac{3}{4}$ $\dfrac{3}{4}$ ☐ $\dfrac{2}{3}$ $\dfrac{1}{3}$ ☐ $\dfrac{4}{8}$

$\dfrac{4}{6}$ ☐ $\dfrac{1}{5}$ $\dfrac{1}{3}$ ☐ $\dfrac{3}{6}$ $\dfrac{2}{4}$ ☐ $\dfrac{5}{8}$

⬛ FRACTIONS AND DECIMALS

[Roblox High School 2]

P1 Maths starts at 9am.

There are 4 students to a table and 10 students, change this **improper fraction** to a **mixed number** to see how many tables will be at full capacity.

$$\frac{10}{4} = \boxed{}\,\frac{\boxed{}}{\boxed{}}$$

A teacher asks for 31 balls to be put into groups of 4.

Express the number of groups there will be using a mixed number.

It's lunchtime! Each bench holds 10 students, change this improper fraction to a mixed number to see how many benches will be at full capacity.

$$\frac{83}{10} = \boxed{}\,\frac{\boxed{}}{\boxed{}}$$

◨ FRACTIONS AND DECIMALS

[Escape Miss Ani—Tron's Detention!]

Continue these **decimal** patterns to stop Miss Ani—Tron glitching.

0.75   0.74   0.73   _____ _____ _____ _____

0.5   0.6   0.7   _____ _____ _____ _____

0.88   0.89   _____ _____ _____ _____

Distract Miss Ani—Tron by **completing the table below** for her to mark.

	$\frac{2}{10}$	0.2	two tenths
	$\frac{}{10}$	0.4	tenths
	$\frac{13}{10}$		thirteen tenths
	$\frac{}{}$	1.4	tenths

FRACTIONS AND DECIMALS

It's working! One of you has found the key to escape, you just need to distract Miss Ani–Tron a little longer!

On the board are two examples of decimals converted to display their fraction equivalent.

Complete the other conversions below as Miss Ani–Tron watches.

$$0.3 = \frac{3}{10} \qquad 0.03 = \frac{3}{100}$$

$$0.1 = \frac{\ }{\ } \qquad 0.7 = \frac{\ }{\ } \qquad 0.06 = \frac{\ }{\ }$$

You did it, you escaped as she was wiping the board clean for the next question!

[Building a dream house in Roblox]

Calculate the perimeters of the rooms below.

Remember; in rectangles opposite sides are equal.

(The perimeter is the distance all the way around the outside of a 2D shape.)

Garage

Shapes aren't drawn to scale

6m

2m

Perimeter = ... + ... + ... + ... = _____ m

Front Room   **Bathroom**

9m   2m

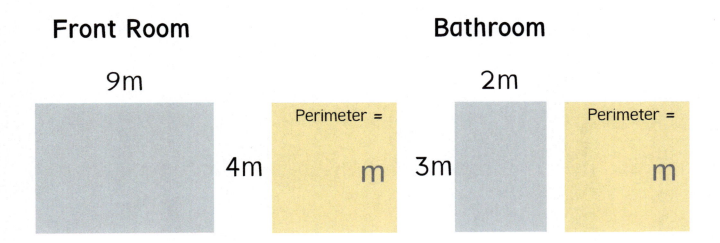

4m   Perimeter = _____ m   3m   Perimeter = _____ m

Calculate the perimeter of the properties below.

Shapes aren't drawn to scale

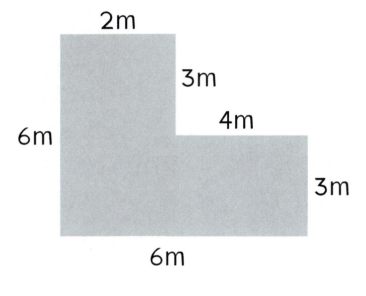

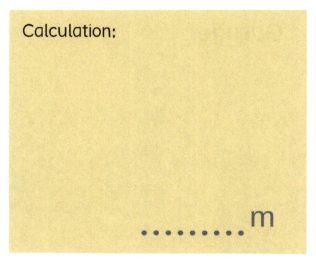

Calculation:

.... m

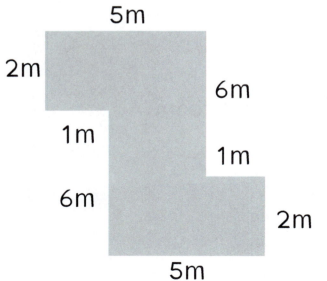

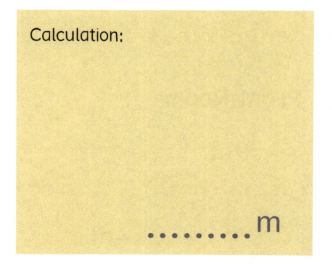

Calculation:

.... m

 AREA AND PERIMETER

Find the **areas** of these shapes.

The area of a shape is the number of unit squares that cover the surface.

Use the answers to form a 6 digit code to escape from Banana Eats.

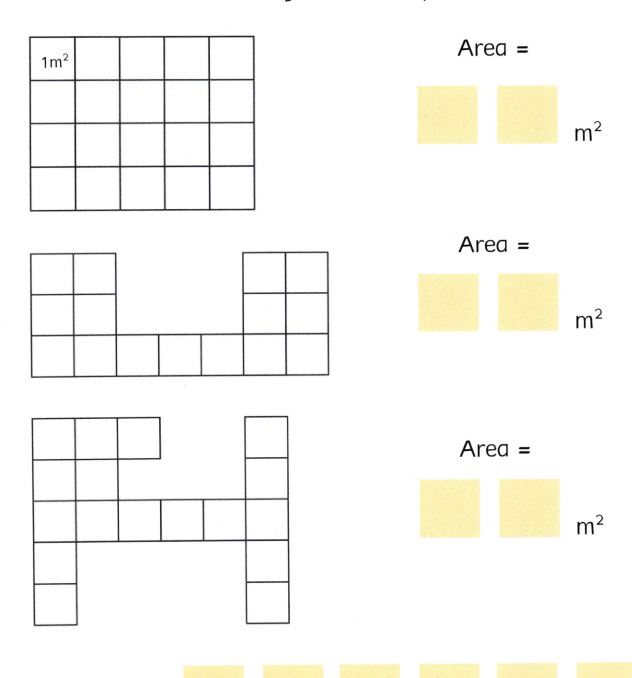

Area =

◻ ◻ m²

Area =

◻ ◻ m²

Area =

◻ ◻ m²

Full escape code ◻ ◻ ◻ ◻ ◻ ◻

This table shows the number of year 4 and year 5 children that play popular Roblox games.

Game	Year 4	Year 5
Brookhaven RP	36	48
Bloxburg	19	32
Adopt Me	41	13
Pet Simulator X	27	29
Anime Fighters	33	47

How many children altogether play Adopt Me?

Which game is the most popular in year 4?

What is the difference between the number of year 4 children who play Bloxburg and the number of year 5 children who play Adopt Me?

STATISTICS

This pictogram shows how many players completed the Escape the Laundromat Obby each day for one week.

Day	Number of players
Monday	🧺🧺🧺🧺
Tuesday	🧺🧺🧺🧺
Wednesday	🧺🧺🧺
Thursday	🧺🧺
Friday	🧺🧺🧺🧺🧺🧺🧺
Saturday	🧺🧺🧺🧺🧺🧺
Sunday	🧺🧺🧺🧺

🧺 = 20 players

Complete the table using the information in the **pictogram**.

Day	Mon	Tues	Weds	Thurs	Fri	Sat	Sun
Number of players							

Circle the day with the fewest completions.

This Tally chart shows the number of SWAT game passes purchased in Jail Break from a Friday to Sunday.

Complete the chart.

Day	Number	Total
Friday	Ж‖‖	
Saturday	Ж Ж Ж	
Sunday		19

How many **more** game passes were sold on Saturday than on Friday?

How many **fewer** game passes were sold on Friday than on Sunday?

How many game passes were sold in **total** at the weekend?

☐ MEASUREMENTS

5 gamers are playing Driving Empire!

Match their **equivalent** driving distances

1500m	1km
1250m	1 1/2 km
1000m	1km 250 m
1750m	2 1/4 km
2250m	1 3/4 km

Carmad2020 drove 4km 600m on Saturday and 1700m on Sunday.

How much further did Carmad2020 drive on Saturday than on Sunday?   metres

Use a ruler to draw a straight line door handle **0.7cm long** onto the car.

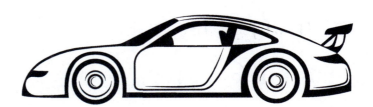

MEASUREMENTS

[Whacky Wizards update]

New potion alert!

Oh no, something has splashed over your conversion table!

Complete it again so you can start creating recipes.

Litres (l)	Millilitres (ml)
0,75	750
	1300
2,30	
7,2	
	990

HarryBlox says 5.05kg of rotten sandwiches is equal to 5500g.

Is this true or false?

SHOPPING FOR MERCH

2 5   6   5   3   1   4   7

Label the coins from 1 – 7 (1 being the coin with the **lowest** value and 7 being the coin with the **highest** value.

If a keyring was £1.77, how could you make up the cost using the coins above?

One Pound   50p   20p 5p 2p = £1.77

A t-shirt costs £4.75, what is your change from

- £5.00   25p
- £10.00   £5.25p

◻ MONEY

Lucas purchased 3 Bloxy Colas, 1 Bloxy Cola is £1.75

How much did Lucas spend in total?

$$x \frac{175}{3}$$
$$\frac{5\ 2\ 5}{2\ X}$$

£5.25

You buy 2 teddys at £2.21 each and a watermelon slice for £0.70

$$70 \quad \begin{array}{r} HTU \\ 442 \\ +\ 70 \\ \hline 5\ 1\ 2 \end{array} \quad x\frac{221}{442} \quad \begin{array}{r} 70 \\ 2+442 \\ \hline 2 \end{array}$$

How much have you spent altogether?

£5.12

Jessie bought 4 pizza slices to give to her friends. Each slice cost £1.10

$$x \frac{110}{4}$$

How much change did she receive if she paid with a £20 note?

£15.60

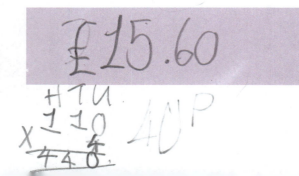

$$\begin{array}{r} HTU \\ x\ 1\ 1\ 0 \\ \hline 4\ 4\ 0 \end{array}$$

It's Friday, there's a new Club Roblox update going live at **twenty to seven.** Circle the analog clock that shows this time.

There is a BIG safari egg update on Adopt Me going live the last day of October.

Will this be the 30th or the 31st?   31

Screen time at the weekend is half an hour in the morning, afternoon and evening.

What time will your screen time end?

Start	End	Start	End	Start	End
09:00	9:30	13:15	13:45	19:45	20:15

0
1

2 gamers play Natural Disaster Survival.

Use the symbols < and > to compare their time spent playing.

3 hours and 20 minutes		190 minutes
1 hour and 45 minutes		145 minutes

	Start	End
AvaGrlxo	10:15am	11:30am
Frankiewins	11:10am	11:55am

Using the table above.

Name the gamer who played for the **shortest** amount of time?

[Adopt Me] Your eggs have hatched!

What is the age of these newborns in days.

Puppy	Mammoth
3 weeks	7 weeks
days	days

What is the age of these pets in months.

Kitty	Giraffe
2 years	4 years 2 months
months	months

A royal egg hatched on the **last day** of June 2021.

When is their 1st birthday?   /   /

ANSWERS

GamerFan22 creates an awesome new avatar and is left with a ⬡ total of **three thousand six hundred and twenty.**

Write out their ⬡ total using numbers.   3620

Friends are comparing their ⬡ totals;

List these numbers in order from smallest to largest.

Robodude – 8092

TwinkleS – 8120

ElitePlus – 6320

Untalkable – 5000

PrestonS – 6100

5000
6100
6320
8092
8120

Write out ElitePlus's total using words.

six thousand three hundred and twenty

You are playing Adopt Me, it's an October Halloween update. You and other players purchase a Shadow Dragon game pass for ⬢ 1000 from the Candy Trading Shop.

How many ⬢ do you and the other players have left?

You	2200	−1000	1200
MrBoost	7830	−1000	6830
Sean100	1350	−1000	350
PinkGamer	9990	−1000	8990

PinkGamer wants to buy 1 Royal Egg and 2 Pink Eggs. Royal eggs are ⬢ 1450 and pink eggs are ⬢ 100.

$$1450$$
$$+ 100$$
$$+ 100$$

What is the total ⬢ cost? 1650

Work at a pizza place

Each item on the menu costs ◉ 100

Player 1, 2 and 3's total spends have been entered incorrectly on the till! Your manager has asked you to round them to the **nearest 100**.

	Total	New Total
Player 1	540	500
Player 2	250	300
Player 3	955	1000

▢ COUNT IN MULTIPLES

Chance to win lucky blocks in The Floor is Lava!

Get the 6 digit winning codes by finding the 3 multiples of each number and entering them into the boxes provided!

Find the 3 multiples of 6

05 (12) 21 (24) (36) 44

Code | 12 | 24 | 36 |

Find the 3 multiples of 7

(28) 13 (56) (77) 82 90

Code | 28 | 56 | 77 |

Find the 3 multiples of 9

17 (45) 52 (63) (81) 22

Code | 45 | 63 | 81 |

◪ COUNT IN MULTIPLES

You've got unlimited 25 skips in the Mega Easy Obby 750 stages.

Count to 750 in multiples of 25.
Fill in the missing stages.

25, 50 , 75 , 100, 125, 150, 175, 200,

225, 250, 275, 300, 325, 350, 375, 400,

425, 450, 475, 500, 525, 550, 575, 600,

625, 650, 675, 700, 725

750

ROMAN NUMERALS

[Building] Empire Roleplay

Your map has 100 forts to help defend your emperor! To command your troops you need to know the Roman Numeral for each fort.

Fill in the missing Roman Numerals on the 100 square below.

I	II	III	IV	V	VI	VII	VIII	IX	X
XI	XII	XIII	XIV	XV	XVI	XVII	XVIII	XIX	XX
XXI	XXII	XXIII	XXIV	XXV	XXVI	XXVII	XXVIII	XXIX	XXX
XXXI	XXXII	XXXIII	XXXIV	XXXV	XXXVI	XXXVII	XXXVIII	XXXIX	XL
XLI	XLII	XLIII	XLIV	XLV	XLVI	XLVII	XLVIII	XLIX	L
LI	LII	LIII	LIV	LV	LVI	LVII	LVIII	LIX	LX
LXI	LXII	LXIII	LXIV	LXV	LXVI	LXVII	LXVIII	LXIX	LXX
LXXI	LXXII	LXXIII	LXXIV	LXXV	LXXVI	LXXVII	LXXVIII	LXXIX	LXXX
LXXXI	LXXXII	LXXXIII	LXXXIV	LXXXV	LXXXVI	LXXXVII	LXXXVIII	LXXXIX	XC
XCI	XCII	XCIII	XCIV	XCV	XCVI	XCVII	XCVIII	XCIX	C

A member of your troop has stolen your opponents map so you can see which forts they are planning to strike.

BUT, they have used numbers!

Use your 100 square to help you find the Roman Numeral equivalent.

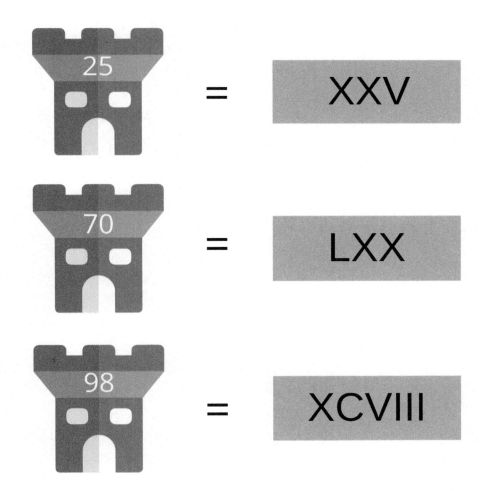

25 = XXV

70 = LXX

98 = XCVIII

Goal: Build a shape obby.

How: Collect the information below needed for coding.

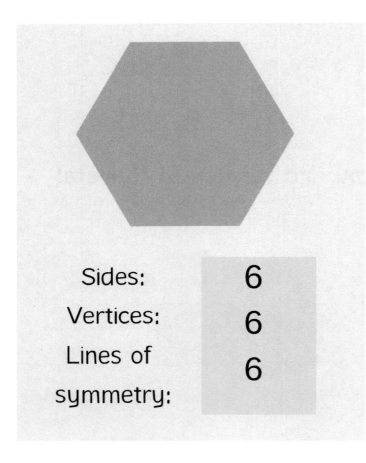

Sides:	6
Vertices:	6
Lines of symmetry:	6

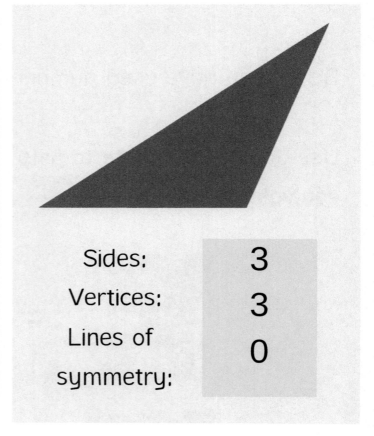

Sides:	3
Vertices:	3
Lines of symmetry:	0

Shape Sudoku

Place these 6 shapes into the blank spaces so that each row, column and **2x2 box** contains one of each shape without repeats.

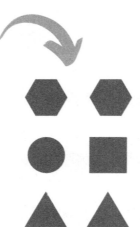

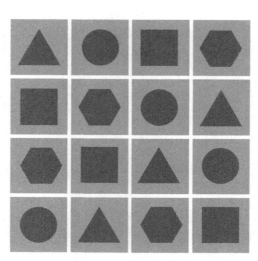

Time to play Theme Park Tycoon 2, you've got your own plot of land to build your theme park on and you have designed 4 roller coasters.

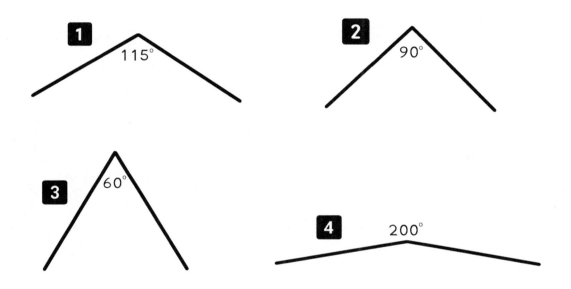

Match the angles of your 4 roller coasters to their angle types.

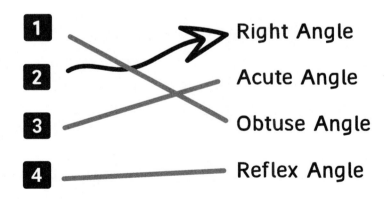

List the angles from **smallest** to **largest**. 60°, 90°, 115°, 200°

Blue team has got some cannons lined up on

Pilfering Pirates!

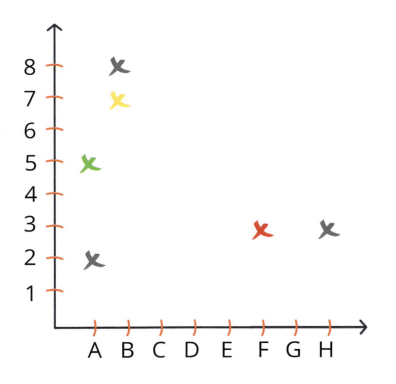

Using the graph, list the coordinates of the 3 ships blue team are aiming for.

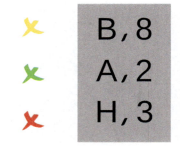

B, 8

A, 2

H, 3

The sea is stormy, the boats have moved.

Plot their new coordinates on the graph.

B,7

A,5

F,3

Which colour boat moved the furthest from their original position?

Green

[Escape the running head]

During the final stages of level 3 you find a green coin and are awarded directions out of the maze!

Follow the instructions below to escape.

Stand still with feet together.

- Turn 2 right angles to the left

- Take 3 step backwards

- Turn 3 right angles to the right

- Take 5 steps forward

- Turn 1 right angle to the left

You've escaped!

The trucks in [Break In (story)] either carry 6, 8 or 11 players. Complete the multiplication wheels below to see how many players join depending on the number of trucks each day between 1–12.

Multiply the numbers by the middle number!

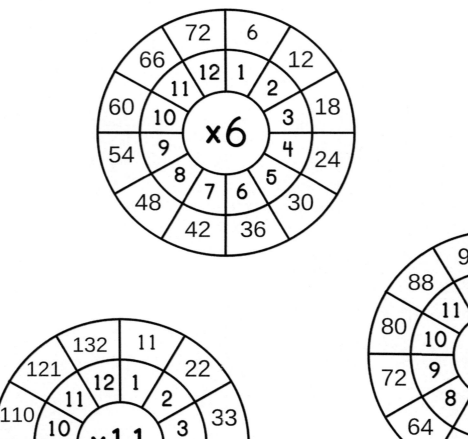

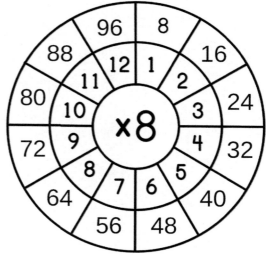

Challenge:

Give yourself 2 minutes to list as many **factor pairs** as you can for the numbers below!

36	12	52
1 x 36	1 x 12	1 x 52
2 x 18	2 x 6	2 x 26
	3 x 4	4 x 13
3 x 12		
4 x 9		
6 x 6		
9 x 4		

GamerGuy31 gets 80 robux daily for keeping his room tidy, how many does he get per week?

560

Each of GamerGuy31's 8 friends have got 4 pet bees ready to make a neon! How many bees are there in total?

32

⬜ MULTIPLICATION

Repeat: I'd rather be playing Roblox, but I need to practice multiplication!

Complete the questions below.

$$
\begin{array}{r}
36 \\
\times\ 5 \\
\hline
180
\end{array}
\qquad
\begin{array}{r}
53 \\
\times\ 4 \\
\hline
212
\end{array}
\qquad
\begin{array}{r}
28 \\
\times\ 8 \\
\hline
224
\end{array}
$$

$$
\begin{array}{r}
46 \\
\times\ 4 \\
\hline
184
\end{array}
\qquad
\begin{array}{r}
22 \\
\times\ 5 \\
\hline
110
\end{array}
\qquad
\begin{array}{r}
12 \\
\times\ 6 \\
\hline
72
\end{array}
$$

$$
\begin{array}{r}
11 \\
\times\ 7 \\
\hline
77
\end{array}
\qquad
\begin{array}{r}
25 \\
\times\ 4 \\
\hline
100
\end{array}
\qquad
\begin{array}{r}
50 \\
\times\ 6 \\
\hline
300
\end{array}
$$

RP : Trapped in the Maths classroom with Baldi.

Baldi won't let you leave until you complete the bus stop division below.

$60 \div 5 =$ 12 $24 \div 3 =$ 8 $48 \div 8 =$ 6

11
6|66

16
4|64

13
7|91

24
3|72

112
5|560

99
8|792

112
3|336

35
4|140

There were 32 students in the class, a quarter escaped! How many made it out?

$32 \div 4 = 8$ 8 students escaped

⬚ ADDITION AND SUBTRACTION

[Car Crusher 2] Shopping Spree!

You want to add 2 new cars to your collection.

Investigate the total costs of the duo vehicles below.

Cherevlo Airvor **2675**

Golf Cart **5102**

Total Cost 7777

Nyssat Salvio **6375**

Cherevlo Alstra **500**

Total Cost 6875

Forter Fabreville **1550**

Golf Cart **5135**

Total Cost 6685

Fita A50 **8075**

Forter Fabreville **1550**

Total Cost 9625

Rylan MK1 **3324**

Cherevlo Airvor **2675**

Total Cost 5999

Forter Fabreville **1550**

Ford MT **1020**

Total Cost 2570

[Meep City Shop] Pick a side

Subtract the cost of each item listed below from your current coin total of <u>9780</u>

Will the answer be on the pink or blue side?

Circle the correct remaining total.

Item	Cost	Coins remaining	
Pogo Stick	3500	(6280)	6820
Unicycle	2000	7000	(7780)
Rollerblades	750	9040	(9030)
Rainbow Sparkler	2500	(7280)	6280
Mystic Wings	1250	(8530)	8930
Bee Wings	950	8800	(8830)

9780 - 3500 = 6280
9780 - 2000 = 7780
9780 - 750 = 9030
9780 - 2500 = 7280
9780 - 1250 = 8530
9780 - 950 = 8830

1500 gamers were asked to pick their favourite game out of Brookhaven, Meep City and Club Roblox.

600 picked Brookhaven, 350 picked Meep City.

How many picked Club Roblox?

$$1500 - 600 - 350 = 550$$

Clubbloxerfan has 7500 coins in Don't Press the Button. They spend 650 on a shrinking potion and 6000 on a flying carpet.

How many coins do they have left?

$$7500 - 6000 - 650 = 850$$

Circle the fraction represented by the black icons.

$$\frac{2}{3} \qquad \frac{1}{2} \qquad \left(\frac{2}{5}\right)$$

The energy bars of 4 players in Blox Fruits are listed in fraction form below. **List them from smallest to largest.**

$$\frac{1}{3} \qquad \frac{1}{10} \qquad \frac{1}{2} \qquad \frac{1}{6}$$

$$\frac{1}{10} \qquad \frac{1}{6} \qquad \frac{1}{3} \qquad \frac{1}{2}$$

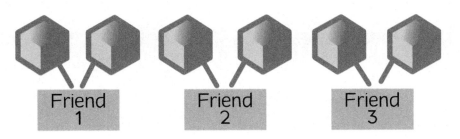

6 lucky blocks are to be shared equally between 3 friends.

What fraction of lucky blocks do they each get?

$$\frac{2}{6} \quad \text{or} \quad \frac{1}{3}$$

[Pizza Factory Tycoon]

2 friends have visited your restaurant, they want to share a pizza. **Circle all the equivalent fractions of** $\frac{1}{2}$

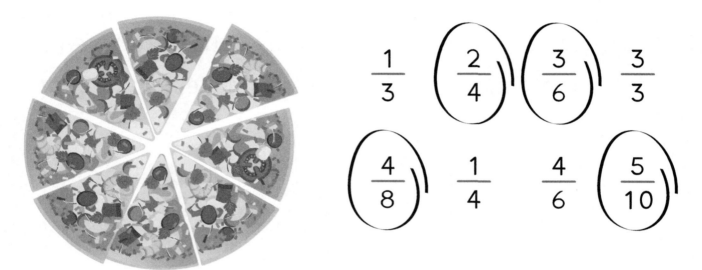

$\frac{1}{3}$ $\boxed{\frac{2}{4}}$ $\boxed{\frac{3}{6}}$ $\frac{3}{3}$

$\boxed{\frac{4}{8}}$ $\frac{1}{4}$ $\frac{4}{6}$ $\boxed{\frac{5}{10}}$

More customers arrive, all pizzas are the same size but the number of slices per pizza varies. Calculate the equivalent fractions below to ensure everyone gets the same amount to eat.

$$\frac{1}{2} = \frac{3}{6} \qquad \frac{3}{6} = \frac{5}{10} \qquad \frac{4}{8} = \frac{6}{12}$$

$$\frac{1}{3} = \frac{2}{6} \qquad \frac{4}{8} = \frac{2}{4} \qquad \frac{3}{4} = \frac{6}{8}$$

◻ FRACTIONS AND DECIMALS

Add these fractions to find out which table ate a **whole** pizza.

Table 1 $\quad \dfrac{1}{7} + \dfrac{5}{7} \quad = \quad \dfrac{6}{7}$

Table 2 $\quad \dfrac{2}{6} + \dfrac{2}{6} \quad = \quad \dfrac{4}{6}$

Table 3 $\quad \dfrac{1}{3} + \dfrac{1}{3} + \dfrac{1}{3} \quad = \quad \dfrac{3}{3}$

Table $\boxed{3}$ finished 1 whole pizza.

There is one big sauce dispenser where customers can get their own pizza dipping sauce. Subtract the fraction of sauce used in a day. **What fraction of sauce is left?**

$$\dfrac{2}{5} - \dfrac{1}{5} = \dfrac{1}{5} \qquad \dfrac{4}{6} - \dfrac{3}{6} = \dfrac{1}{6}$$

PiggyFan11 and friends are all comparing how much pizza they have eaten, but their pizzas all had different amounts of slices. This means their fractions all have different denominators.

Using the symbols < and > compare the pizza fractions to see who ate the most.

Tip: Draw pizza shapes and shade in the fractions to help you to compare!

$$\frac{1}{2} < \frac{3}{4} \qquad \frac{3}{4} > \frac{2}{3} \qquad \frac{1}{3} < \frac{4}{8}$$

$$\frac{4}{6} > \frac{1}{5} \qquad \frac{1}{3} < \frac{3}{6} \qquad \frac{2}{4} < \frac{5}{8}$$

⬚ FRACTIONS AND DECIMALS

[Roblox High School 2]

P1 Maths starts at 9am.

There are 4 students to a table and 10 students, change this **improper fraction** to a **mixed number** to see how many tables will be at full capacity.

$$\frac{10}{4} = 2\frac{2}{4}$$

A teacher asks for 31 balls to be put into groups of 4.

Express the number of groups there will be using a mixed number.

$$7\frac{3}{4}$$

It's lunchtime! Each bench holds 10 students, change this improper fraction to a mixed number to see how many benches will be at full capacity.

$$\frac{83}{10} = 8\frac{3}{10}$$

⬚ FRACTIONS AND DECIMALS

[Escape Miss Ani—Tron's Detention!]

Continue these **decimal** patterns to stop Miss Ani—Tron glitching.

0.75   0.74   0.73   __0.72__   __0.71__   __0.70__   __0.69__

0.5   0.6   0.7   __0.8__   __0.9__   __1__   __1.1__

0.88   0.89   __0.90__   __0.91__   __0.92__   __0.93__

Distract Miss Ani—Tron by **completing the table below**
for her to mark.

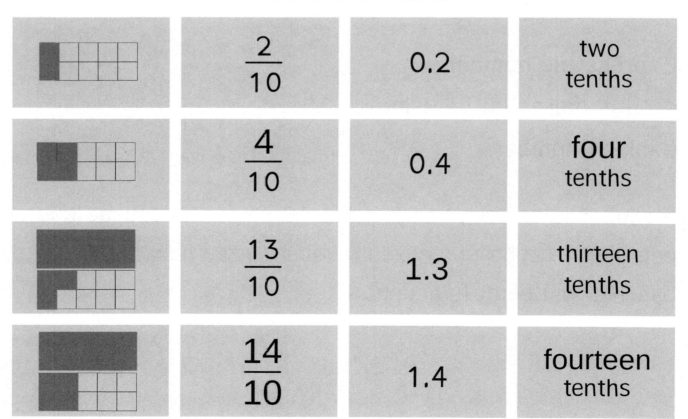

	$\frac{2}{10}$	0.2	two tenths
	$\frac{4}{10}$	0.4	four tenths
	$\frac{13}{10}$	1.3	thirteen tenths
	$\frac{14}{10}$	1.4	fourteen tenths

It's working! One of you has found the key to escape, you just need to distract Miss Ani—Tron a little longer!

On the board are two examples of decimals converted to display their fraction equivalent.

Complete the other conversions below as Miss Ani—Tron watches.

$$0.3 = \frac{3}{10} \qquad 0.03 = \frac{3}{100}$$

$$0.1 = \frac{1}{10} \qquad 0.7 = \frac{7}{10} \qquad 0.06 = \frac{6}{100}$$

You did it, you escaped as she was wiping the board clean for the next question!

⬚ AREA AND PERIMETER

[Building a dream house in Roblox]

Calculate the perimeters of the rooms below.

Remember; in rectangles opposite sides are equal.

(The perimeter is the distance all the way around the outside of a 2D shape.)

Shapes aren't drawn to scale

Garage

6m

2m

Perimeter = $\underline{6}$ + $\underline{2}$ + $\underline{6}$ + $\underline{2}$ **16m**

Front Room

9m

4m

Perimeter =

9+4 x 2

26m

Bathroom

2m

3m

Perimeter =

3+2 x 2

10m

AREA AND PERIMETER

Calculate the perimeter of the properties below.

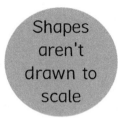

Shapes aren't drawn to scale

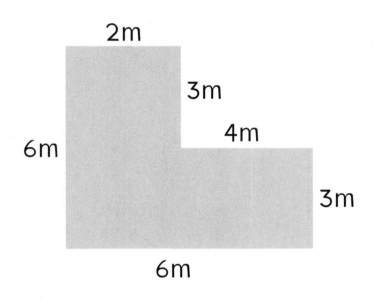

2m
3m
4m
6m
3m
6m

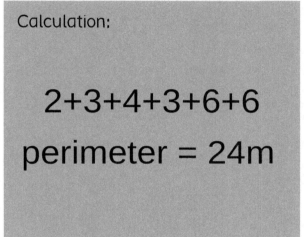

Calculation:

2+3+4+3+6+6

perimeter = 24m

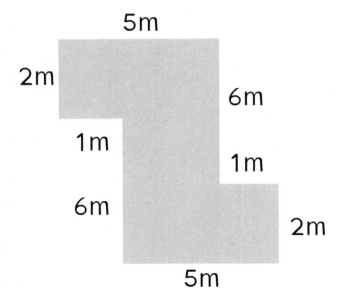

5m
2m
6m
1m
1m
6m
2m
5m

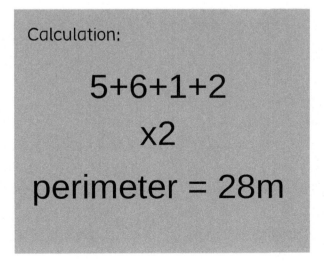

Calculation:

5+6+1+2

x2

perimeter = 28m

◻ AREA AND PERIMETER

Find the **areas** of these shapes.

The area of a shape is the number of unit squares that cover the surface.

Use the answers to form a 6 digit code to escape from Banana Eats.

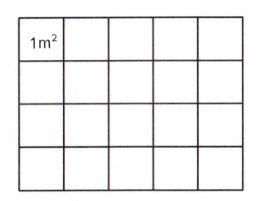

Area =

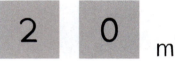

$$2 \quad 0 \quad m^2$$

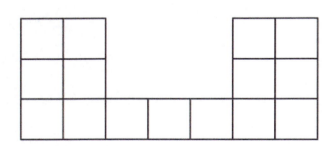

Area =

$$1 \quad 5 \quad m^2$$

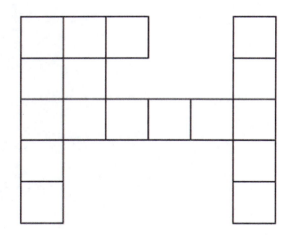

Area =

$$1 \quad 7 \quad m^2$$

Full escape code   2   0   1   5   1   7

This table shows the number of year 4 and year 5 children that play popular Roblox games.

Game	Year 4	Year 5
Brookhaven RP	36	48
Bloxburg	19	32
Adopt Me	41	13
Pet Simulator X	27	29
Anime Fighters	33	47

How many children altogether play Adopt Me? **54**

Which game is the most popular in year 4? **Adopt Me**

What is the difference between the number of year 4 children who play Bloxburg and the number of year 5 children who play Adopt Me? **6**

This pictogram shows how many players completed the Escape the Laundromat Obby each day for one week.

 = 20 players

Day	Number of players
Monday	🧺 🧺 🧺 🧺
Tuesday	🧺 🧺 🧺 🧺
Wednesday	🧺 🧺 🧺
Thursday	🧺 🧺
Friday	🧺 🧺 🧺 🧺 🧺 🧺 🧺
Saturday	🧺 🧺 🧺 🧺 🧺
Sunday	🧺 🧺 🧺 🧺

Complete the table using the information in the **pictogram**.

Day	Mon	Tues	Weds	Thurs	Fri	Sat	Sun
Number of players	70	80	50	40	140	110	70

(Thurs is circled)

Circle the day with the fewest completions.

This Tally chart shows the number of SWAT game passes purchased in Jail Break from a Friday to Sunday.

Complete the chart.

Day	Number	Total
Friday	ⅲ |||	8
Saturday	ⅲ ⅲ ⅲ	15
Sunday	ⅲ ⅲ ⅲ ||||	19

How many **more** game passes were sold on Saturday than on Friday? 7

How many **fewer** game passes were sold on Friday than on Sunday? 11

How many game passes were sold in **total** at the weekend? 34

5 gamers are playing Driving Empire!

Match their equivalent driving distances

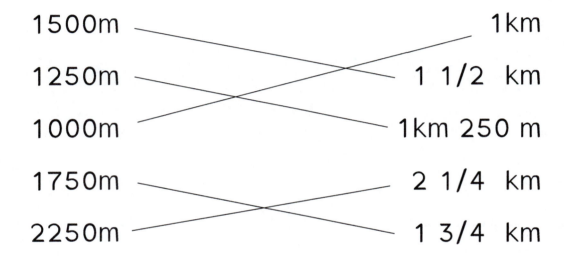

1500m	1km
1250m	1 1/2 km
1000m	1km 250 m
1750m	2 1/4 km
2250m	1 3/4 km

Carmad2020 drove 4km 600m on Saturday and 1700m on Sunday.

How much further did Carmad2020 drive on Saturday than on Sunday?   4600 - 1700   2900 metres

Use a ruler to draw a straight line door handle **0.7cm long** onto the car.

7mm line

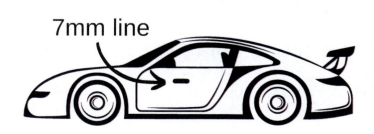

[Whacky Wizards update]

New potion alert!

Oh no, something has splashed over your conversion table!

Complete it again so you can start creating recipes.

Litres (l)	Millilitres (ml)
0.75	750
1.30	1300
2.30	2300
7.2	7200
0.99	990

HarryBlox says 5.05kg of rotten sandwiches is equal to 5500g.

Is this true or false?   False, 5.05kg = 5050g

SHOPPING FOR MERCH

| 2 | 6 | 5 | 3 | 1 | 4 | 7 |

Label the coins from 1 – 7 (1 being the coin with the **lowest** value and 7 being the coin with the **highest** value.

If a keyring was £1.77, how could you make up the cost using the coins above?

A t-shirt costs £4.75, what is your change from

- £5   5 - 4.75 = 0.25 = 25p

- £10   10 - 4.75 = 5.25 = £5.25

Lucas purchased 3 Bloxy Colas, 1 Bloxy Cola is £1.75

How much did Lucas spend in total?

$$1.75 \times 3 = £5.25$$

You buy 2 teddys at £2.21 each and a watermelon slice for £0.70

How much have you spent altogether?

$$2.21 \times 2 = 4.42 + 0.70 = £5.12$$

Jessie bought 4 pizza slices to give to her friends. Each slice cost £1.10

How much change did she receive if she paid with a £20 note?

$$1.10 \times 4 = 4.40 \quad £20 - 4.40 = £15.60 \text{ change}$$

It's Friday, there's a new Club Roblox update going live at **twenty to seven.** Circle the analog clock that shows this time.

There is a BIG safari egg update on Adopt Me going live the <u>last</u> day of October.

Will this be the 30th or the 31st? 31st

Screen time at the weekend is half an hour in the morning, afternoon and evening.

What time will your screen time end?

Start	End	Start	End	Start	End
09:00	09:30	13:15	13:45	19:45	20:15

2 gamers play Natural Disaster Survival.

Use the symbols < and > to compare their time spent playing.

3 hours and 20 minutes   >   190 minutes

1 hour and 45 minutes   <   145 minutes

	Start	End
AvaGrlxo	10:15am	11:30am
Frankiewins	11:10am	11:55am

Using the table above.

Name the gamer who played for the **shortest** amount of time?

Frankiewins

[Adopt Me] Your eggs have hatched!

What is the age of these newborns in days.

Puppy	Mammoth
3 weeks	7 weeks
21 days	**49** days

What is the age of these pets in months.

Kitty	Giraffe
2 years	4 years 2 months
24 months	**50** months

A royal egg hatched on the **last day** of June 2021.

When is their 1st birthday?   **30 / 06 / 2022**

Printed in Great Britain
by Amazon